Oxford Read and Imag...

G000161435

What's So Funny?

By Paul Shipton

Illustrated by Carl Pearce

Activities by Hannah Fish

Contents

OXFORD

UNIVERSITY PRESS

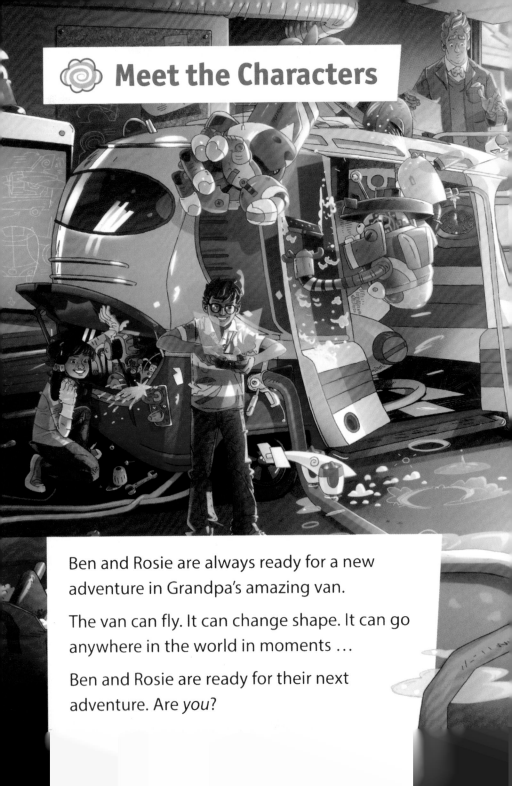

Meet the Characters

Ben and Rosie are always ready for a new adventure in Grandpa's amazing van.

The van can fly. It can change shape. It can go anywhere in the world in moments …

Ben and Rosie are ready for their next adventure. Are *you*?

Grandpa Ben and Rosie's grandfather, a scientist and inventor

Clunk Grandpa's robot

Ben Rosie's brother

Rosie Ben's sister

Max and his sister Alice Ben and Rosie's friends

Rick Richards a scientist

Imagine!

One day, there is an accident in town, and everyone starts to smile and laugh. Why is everyone laughing? What happens when the laughter stops? Read *What's So Funny?* and find out.

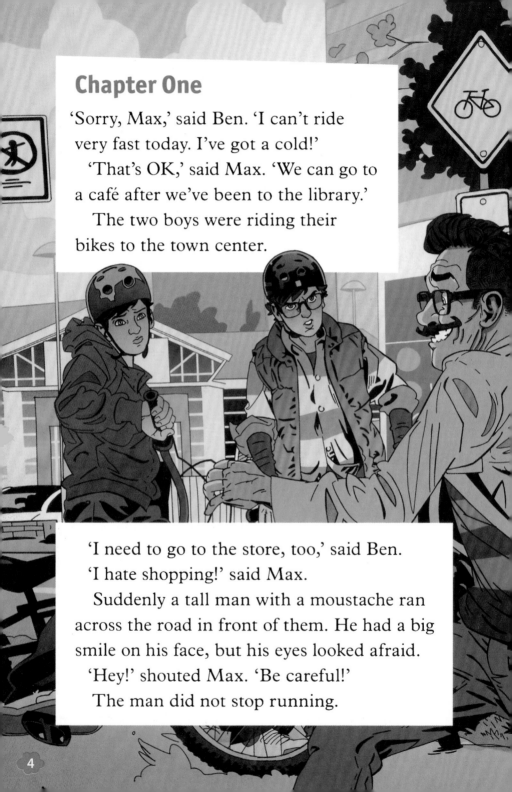

Chapter One

'Sorry, Max,' said Ben. 'I can't ride very fast today. I've got a cold!'

'That's OK,' said Max. 'We can go to a café after we've been to the library.'

The two boys were riding their bikes to the town center.

'I need to go to the store, too,' said Ben.

'I hate shopping!' said Max.

Suddenly a tall man with a moustache ran across the road in front of them. He had a big smile on his face, but his eyes looked afraid.

'Hey!' shouted Max. 'Be careful!'

The man did not stop running.

When they turned the corner, Ben and Max could see a crowd of people in the street.

'We'll have to walk from here,' said Ben.

They got off their bikes and locked them at the side of the street.

'Something has happened,' said Max. He pointed down the street. 'I think that I can see smoke.'

'Maybe there's been an accident,' said Ben.

A moment later, they heard the sound of a police car. The crowd started to move and now the boys could see more.

➔ Go to page 36 for activities.

'Look – there *has* been an accident!' said Max. 'That tanker hit a street light.'

At first Ben was worried about the driver. Had he been hurt? Then he saw a man in a blue uniform. He was talking to a police officer. The badge on the man's shirt had the same words that were on the side of the tanker – HAPPY WORLD.

One of the police officers was looking at the side of the tanker.

'There's a hole in it,' said Ben nervously. 'And something's coming out – is that *gas*?'

Ben turned to run, but Max stopped him.

'It's OK,' he said. 'Look – that police officer's laughing now. There's nothing to be frightened about.' Max smiled. 'You worry too much, Ben,' he said. 'It's a beautiful day. Let's go shopping!'

'But there's been an accident,' said Ben. 'And you hate shopping, Max!'

Max's smile grew bigger. Then, Ben noticed that Max was not the only person who was smiling. *Everyone* was smiling – the police officers, the tanker driver, all the people in the street …

What was happening here?

→ Go to page 37 for activities.

Chapter Two

Ben's cold was getting worse. His head hurt and he felt awful.

'Let's just go home,' he said. 'We can come back to town tomorrow.'

But Max didn't move. He started laughing quietly.

'What's so funny?' Ben asked. 'Why are you laughing?'

Max laughed more at that. Ben looked around and saw that again Max wasn't alone. Everyone except Ben was laughing. The police officer at the back of the tanker was holding his stomach and laughing. The sound of laughter all around Ben grew louder and louder.

Max had to sit down because he couldn't stop laughing.

Quickly, Ben pulled out his cell phone. When strange things happened, there was only one person to call …

'Hello, Grandpa?' Ben said into the phone.

After Ben explained everything, Grandpa said, 'I already know about this problem.'

'How?' asked Ben.

'Your sister is here with me. She just came home from town with Alice,' said Grandpa. 'Rosie hasn't stopped laughing since she arrived.' Grandpa sounded worried. 'Just come home, Ben. I'm going to find out what's happening. Until then, I want you to be safe.'

→ Go to page 38 for activities.

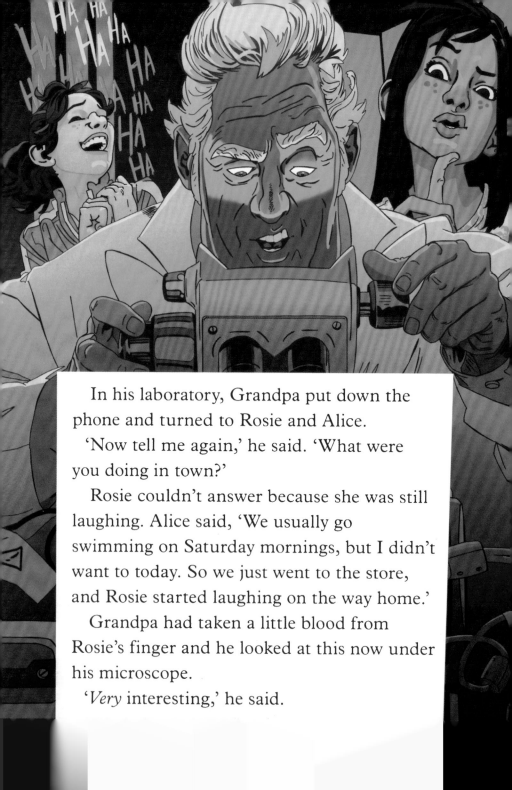

In his laboratory, Grandpa put down the phone and turned to Rosie and Alice.

'Now tell me again,' he said. 'What were you doing in town?'

Rosie couldn't answer because she was still laughing. Alice said, 'We usually go swimming on Saturday mornings, but I didn't want to today. So we just went to the store, and Rosie started laughing on the way home.'

Grandpa had taken a little blood from Rosie's finger and he looked at this now under his microscope.

'*Very* interesting,' he said.

'What's interesting?' asked Alice.

'There are lots of white blood cells in Rosie's blood,' explained Grandpa. 'The body makes more of them to fight off microbes that shouldn't be in the blood.' He turned to Rosie. 'You're *sick*.'

'Really?' said Alice.

Suddenly there was a noise – somebody was knocking at the door.

'Clunk, please see who's there,' said Grandpa.

A moment later, they heard the sound of more laughter. At the door there was a tall man with a moustache and big, frightened eyes. He was laughing and laughing.

→ Go to page 39 for activities.

Chapter Three

The man with the moustache couldn't speak, but he pointed at an identity card on his jacket.

'It says that his name is Rick Richards,' Clunk read from the card. 'He's a scientist at the company Happy World.' Clunk looked up. 'That's the company whose tanker had the accident.'

Grandpa was studying the man. 'Rick Richards … I know you,' he said. 'We worked together at the university years ago!'

Rick nodded his head.

'And you're here because you need help?'

Rick was crying with laughter now, but he nodded again.

Clunk was looking online. 'Happy World is a scientific company,' he said. 'Their website says "Happy World makes the world a happier place through science."'

Grandpa turned to Rick. 'Did your company make what was in that tanker?' he asked. 'Is that what made everyone sick?'

Rick nodded twice.

'And does your company also have a cure?' asked Grandpa.

This time Rick shook his head as he laughed – *no*.

Grandpa understood. 'So you want me to help? To make a cure?'

When Rick nodded again, Grandpa turned to Clunk. 'Quick! We have lots of work to do.'

→ Go to page 40 for activities.

'I have a question,' said Alice, who was sitting and holding Rosie's hand. 'Ben and I aren't laughing. Why aren't we sick? Why aren't *you* laughing, Grandpa?'

'I'm not sure,' said Grandpa. 'Maybe something in our DNA kept us safe … I won't know until I've studied the microbe more.'

Grandpa worked and worked. He only looked up when he heard a voice from the other side of the room: 'Let me help.'

It was Rick Richards and he wasn't laughing now …

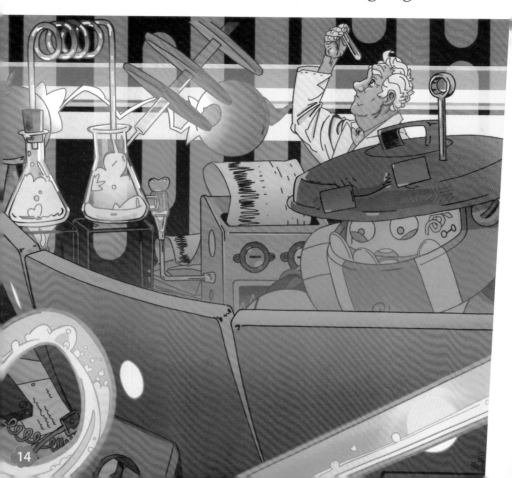

'So what was inside that
tanker, Rick?' Grandpa asked.

'A new gas called Shop Happy,' Rick answered.
'We planned to sell it to stores. When people breathe
in the gas, they feel happy for a short time. And when
people feel happy …'

' … they shop more and spend more money,'
said Grandpa.

'Is a gas like that *safe*?' asked Alice.

'We thought that our gas was safe,' said Rick. 'But
then it changed. It got stronger. The tanker was
taking it somewhere to be destroyed safely. Then the
accident happened …'

→ Go to page 41 for activities.

Chapter Four

'Maybe we don't need a cure now,' Grandpa said to Rick. '*You've* stopped laughing. Maybe your blood cells have killed the microbes from the gas. Perhaps it will be the same for everybody else.'

Rick shook his head sadly. 'The laughter is just the start of the illness,' he said. 'After that –' He started to yawn.

'After that you get tired?' guessed Grandpa.

'Very, very tired,' agreed Rick. Suddenly he couldn't keep his eyes open. He was on the floor now. 'I just need a quick sleep …'

'You can't sleep now!' cried Alice, but it was too late – Rick was already asleep.

'I don't understand,' said Alice. 'Why is Rosie still laughing?'

'Rick must have been the first person to breathe in the gas,' said Grandpa. 'Rosie will probably stop soon.'

He was right – a few minutes later Rosie stopped laughing, too.

'Are you feeling OK?' Alice asked her friend.

'Yes, thanks,' answered Rosie. 'I'm just tired.'

Grandpa looked worried.

'What's wrong?' Alice asked him.

'The Shop Happy microbe is changing all the time,' he said. 'We don't know what happens to people when they wake up.'

→ Go to page 42 for activities.

Suddenly, Grandpa sneezed.

'Wait a minute,' Rosie said. 'Are *you* sick, Grandpa?'

'Well, I had a cold a few days ago,' said Grandpa. 'Ben caught it from me. Why do you ask?'

'Because Alice has a cold, too,' said Rosie. She started to yawn.

'It's true,' agreed Alice. 'That's why I didn't want to go swimming today.'

Rosie yawned again. 'Maybe you three didn't catch the laughing illness because you all have colds!'

Grandpa gave Rosie a big smile. 'That's *brilliant*!' he said. 'And if you're right, I think that I can make a cure for this strange illness!'

Rosie smiled weakly and sat down. 'I'm tired now. Really, really …' Seconds later her head was on the table — she was asleep.

Alice, Grandpa, and Clunk worked hard. When Grandpa told her a chemical, Alice ran to find it on the shelves.

At last Grandpa said, 'It's almost ready. Now we just need salt – lots and lots of salt.'

Alice looked on the shelves. 'There isn't *any* salt here,' she said. 'Can Clunk go and get some?'

'I need Clunk here to help me,' said Grandpa.

'Then how will we get salt?' asked Alice.

'Ben can get it,' said Grandpa.

→ Go to page 43 for activities.

Chapter Five

The town was quiet and still.

Ben felt more alone than ever before. Everybody was sleeping.

Ben had tried to persuade Max to come home, but Max didn't want to go. Now Max was sleeping, and Ben couldn't wake him up.

Ben looked around. The only noise was the sound of hundreds of snores.

Suddenly there was another sound – his cell phone!

'Hello?' said Ben into the phone. 'Is that you, Grandpa?'

Grandpa quickly explained what he needed – a big bag of salt!

'No problem,' said Ben. 'I'm close to the supermarket now.'

Inside the supermarket, more people were sleeping. Ben found a big bag of salt. He left some money at the till and then put the heavy bag on one shoulder.

'I have it, Grandpa,' he said into the phone. 'I'm coming home now.'

Grandpa didn't answer.

'Grandpa?' said Ben. He could hear another voice on the phone, a man's voice. Ben didn't know what the man was saying, but he sounded angry.

'Grandpa!' Ben said again. 'Are you OK?'

The shouts at the other end of the phone got louder.

→ Go to page 44 for activities.

The person who was shouting was Rick Richards.
He had woken up while Grandpa was still on the phone.

At first he had looked around slowly. As Rick saw
all the equipment and chemicals in Grandpa's
laboratory, his face got redder and redder. 'Are you
trying to steal my work?' he said angrily.

'Of course not,' said Clunk.

Rick got even angrier. 'A robot!' he shouted.
'A robot's trying to steal my ideas!' He jumped up
and ran at Clunk.

'Help!' said Clunk.

Alice and Grandpa watched as Rick ran after the
little robot.

'This must be the next part of the illness,' said Alice. 'First people laugh, then they sleep. And when they wake up, they're *angry*!'

'Come here!' shouted Rick, but the robot was faster than he looked. Clunk ran into a little room next to the laboratory. Rick followed him. Moments later, Clunk ran out and locked the door behind him.

'LET ME OUT!' shouted Rick.

Grandpa put the phone to his ear again. 'Ben,' he said. 'Please get home quickly. Soon everybody is going to wake up. And they're going to be *very* angry …'

➜ Go to page 45 for activities.

Chapter Six

When Grandpa put down the phone, Alice was looking at him.

'Aren't you worried about Ben?' she asked.

'Yes, of course,' said Grandpa.

'Then … why are you smiling?' asked Alice.

The smile didn't leave Grandpa's face. 'Rosie was right,' he said. 'You and Ben didn't catch the illness because you already have colds. I *had* a cold a few days ago, but it has almost gone. The Shop Happy microbe took longer to grow in me, but now I have the laughing illness, too.'

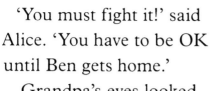

'You must fight it!' said Alice. 'You have to be OK until Ben gets home.'

Grandpa's eyes looked worried but his smile got bigger. 'I'll try,' he said.

Ben was walking to the door of the supermarket. The bag of salt was heavy and he already felt tired.

He could still hear snores, but now there were other sounds, too, as people started to wake up. One woman said, 'What's happening? Why's everyone on the ground?'

Then a louder voice from inside the supermarket shouted, 'Stop that boy! He's stealing something!'

→ Go to page 46 for activities.

Ben turned and saw two supermarket workers who were running toward him.

'I left some money by the till!' Ben shouted.

The supermarket workers didn't seem to hear him. Ben ran.

Somebody had parked a car near the supermarket doors. Quickly, Ben ran behind it and hid.

Soon he heard two angry voices:

'Where did he go?'

'I don't know.'

Ben looked around. On the street, more people were waking up. Soon they were going to see him. How could he get home?

His bike! Ben had locked his bike not far from here! He picked up the bag of salt again and ran.

Ben started to cough, but he didn't stop running.

Behind him one of the supermarket workers shouted, 'I see him!'

A man shouted, 'Get that boy!' There were more angry shouts but Ben tried not to listen.

He was at his bike now. Quickly, he put the bag in the basket and then jumped on the bike.

Ben heard the sound of lots of feet on the sidewalk as people ran toward him.

'Come back, you!'

But the bike was already moving fast and Ben did not look back again.

→ Go to page 47 for activities.

Chapter Seven

In Grandpa's laboratory, Alice was getting more and more frightened. Ben wasn't home yet. Rick Richards was hitting the door with his hand and shouting, 'Let me out!'

Rosie was still sleeping, but for how long?

Alice watched Grandpa. He was trying hard not to laugh as he worked. It was getting more and more difficult. Soon he was laughing quietly. His laughs got louder and longer.

When Grandpa's hands started to shake too much, Clunk helped him to mix the chemicals.

Suddenly the door opened. 'I'm home!' shouted Ben.

The salt was the last thing that Grandpa needed for the cure. He was laughing too much to speak now, but Clunk knew what to do. Quickly, the robot opened the bag and started to add the salt to the other chemicals.

'Hey!' shouted Rick Richards. 'I said … LET … ME … OUT!'

On this last word, Rick pushed open the closed door. He looked angrier and more dangerous than ever as he stood in the doorway.

'Now where's that robot?' he shouted.

→ Go to page 48 for activities.

When Rick ran at him, Clunk jumped back. Some of the liquid in the container fell on the floor.

After that, a few things happened very quickly. Grandpa stopped laughing. Also, Rick stopped running at Clunk. He looked down at his hands and said, 'Er … what am I doing?'

And Rosie's eyes opened at last. She looked around the room slowly and then she said, 'Can someone tell me what's happening?'

'It's a long story,' said Ben.

'There's no time to tell it now,' said Grandpa. 'As soon as people breathe in this cure, it will kill the Shop Happy microbes in their blood. Everyone will be better immediately!'

Ten minutes later, the van was full of containers of the cure, and Clunk was behind the driver's wheel.

'You know what to do, Clunk,' said Grandpa.

The robot nodded.

'What is he going to do?' asked Rick.

'He's going to fly over the town,' said Grandpa. 'There's a machine at the back of the van that can spray the cure into the air. Everyone in town will breathe it.'

A moment later, the van was moving and then it went up into the air. WHOOSH!

→ Go to page 49 for activities.

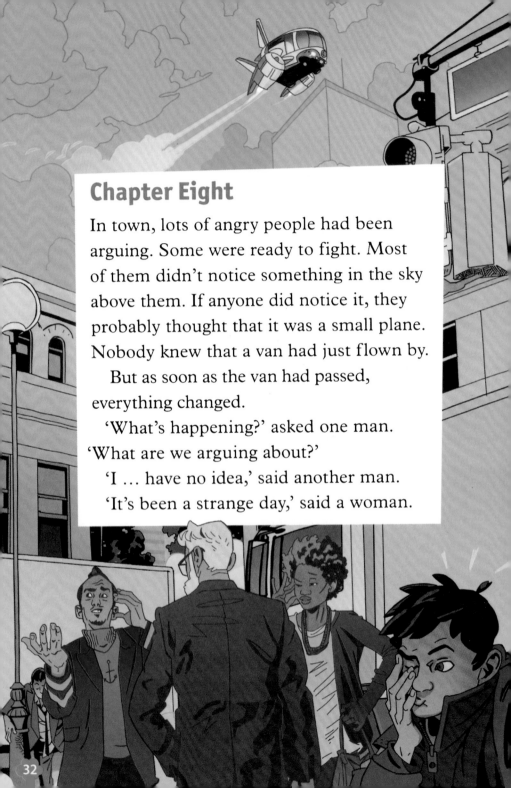

Chapter Eight

In town, lots of angry people had been arguing. Some were ready to fight. Most of them didn't notice something in the sky above them. If anyone did notice it, they probably thought that it was a small plane. Nobody knew that a van had just flown by.

But as soon as the van had passed, everything changed.

'What's happening?' asked one man. 'What are we arguing about?'

'I … have no idea,' said another man.

'It's been a strange day,' said a woman.

When Max heard that, he had to agree – it *had* been a strange day. He couldn't remember much about it, so he didn't really know what had happened. But he knew who to ask. Max pulled out his cell phone and called his best friend.

When he answered, Ben quickly explained everything. 'Shall I come into town and meet you?' he said. 'We can still go shopping, if you want.'

'Shopping?' said Max. 'No! I hate shopping!'

Ben smiled. His friend was back.

→ Go to page 50 for activities.

Rick was moving to the door. 'Thank you,' he said to Grandpa. 'I knew that you'd help us.'

Grandpa smiled. 'Wait, Rick,' he said. 'What's your company going to do now with the Shop Happy gas?'

'I told you,' said Rick. 'We're going to destroy it.' He didn't look Grandpa in the eyes.

'Then will you make a new, *better* gas?' asked Grandpa. 'Another microbe that people will breathe in safely?'

Rick was quiet. At last he said, 'If we can get it right, Shop Happy will be fantastic. Just think ... If stores and towns use it, people will feel better. *Everyone* will be happier.'

'And happier people buy more things,' said Grandpa.
'That's terrible!' said Rosie.

'It's also illegal,' said Grandpa. 'And the police will
be very interested to hear about it.' He had his phone
in his hand. 'Shall I call them, Rick? Or would you
prefer to?'

Rick thought about all the money from his
important job with Happy World. Then he thought
about what was right. 'Give me the phone, please,'
he said quietly.

While Rick was on the phone, Alice turned to Rosie.
'I still have a cold,' she said. 'Shall we stay at home?
There's a funny movie on TV.'

'No, thanks!' said Rosie. 'I've laughed enough today!'

→ Go to page 51 for activities.

Activities for pages 4–5

1 **Read the sentences. Choose and write the correct words.**

1 Ben and Max were ___riding___ their bikes to the town center.

   a pushing **b** ~~riding~~ **c** driving

2 Ben needed to _____ to the stores.

   a go **b** going **c** driving

3 A man ran _____ the road in front of them.

   a through **b** over **c** across

4 The boys _____ see a crowd of people in the street.

   a must **b** could **c** should

5 The boys _____ their bikes at the side of the street.

   a shut **b** locked **c** kept

6 Max thought _____ he could see smoke.

   a that **b** what **c** which

7 Then they heard the sound _____ a police car.

   a at **b** for **c** of

Talk **What do you think had happened?
Tell a friend your ideas.**

1 Find and write the words.

1 This is a special truck that is used
   to carry a liquid or a gas.   t <u>a</u> <u>n</u> <u>k</u> <u>e</u> <u>r</u>

2 This is what you do with your mouth
   when you are happy.   s __ __ __ __

3 This is something that happens, but
   wasn't supposed to.   a __ __ __ __ __ __ __

4 This isn't a liquid or a solid. Oxygen is this.   g __ __

5 These are special clothes that some
   people have to wear at work.   u __ __ __ __ __ __

6 This is something you put on your clothes.   b __ __ __ __

2 Circle the correct words.

1 A tanker had hit a **building** / (**street light**).

2 Ben saw a man in a **blue** / **red** uniform.

3 The badge on the man's shirt said Happy **Man** / **World**.

4 There was a hole in the **front** / **side** of the tanker.

5 **Something** / **Nothing** was coming out of the hole.

6 The police officer was **shouting** / **laughing**.

7 Then Ben noticed that everyone was **smiling** / **talking**.

Why was everyone smiling?

Talk **Tell a friend your ideas.**

Activities for pages 8–9

1 Choose and write the correct words.

Ben's cold was ¹___getting___ worse. He wanted ²_____
home. But Max started laughing ³_____. Then Ben
⁴_____ around and saw that ⁵_____ was
laughing. The police officer ⁶_____ the side of the
tanker was holding ⁷_____ stomach and laughing.
Ben called Grandpa and ⁸_____ everything. Grandpa
already knew about the problem because Rosie ⁹_____
stopped laughing since coming home ¹⁰_____ town.

1 **a** got **b** ~~getting~~ **c** get **d** gets

2 **a** goes **b** going **c** go **d** to go

3 **a** quietly **b** quiet **c** quieter **d** quietest

4 **a** saw **b** watched **c** looked **d** was

5 **a** one **b** anyone **c** someone **d** everyone

6 **a** to **b** at **c** of **d** in

7 **a** him **b** its **c** his **d** he's

8 **a** explained **b** explaining **c** explains **d** explain

9 **a** couldn't **b** didn't **c** hadn't **d** wasn't

10 **a** from **b** for **c** of **d** do

Activities for pages 10–11

1 Circle the correct answers.

1 Who did Grandpa speak to on the phone?

Max (Ben) Rosie

2 What were Rosie and Alice doing in town?

laughing   swimming   shopping

3 When did Rosie start laughing?

on the way home   in town   in a store

4 What did Grandpa look at under his microscope?

Rosie   Rosie's blood   Rosie's finger

5 What was there a lot of in Rosie's blood?

red blood cells   white blood cells   microbes

6 Why does the body make white blood cells?

to fight off microbes   to make you sick
to make more blood

7 Who went to the door?

Grandpa   Alice   Clunk

8 Who was at the door?

Ben   a tall man   a police officer

Talk **Who was the man at the door?**
Tell a friend your ideas.

Activities for pages 12–13

1 **Complete each sentence so it means the same as the first. Use no more than three words.**

1 Happy World was the company whose tanker had the accident.

The tanker ___that had___ the accident was from the company Happy World.

2 Happy World makes the world a happier place through science.

Happy World uses science _____ the world a happier place.

3 Did your company make what was in that tanker?

Was it your company that _____ what was in that tanker?

4 We have a lot of work to do.

There is a lot of work for _____ to do.

2 **Write yes or no.**

1 The man with the moustache couldn't speak. ___yes___

2 The man's name was Rick Richards. _____

3 Rick Richards was a tanker driver. _____

4 Grandpa used to teach Rick Richards. _____

5 Happy World made what was in the tanker. _____

6 What was in the tanker made everyone sick. _____

7 Happy World had a cure for the illness. _____

1 **Choose the correct answers.**

1 Alice, Ben, and Grandpa were the only ones not laughing.

a Right   **b** Wrong   **c** Doesn't say

2 Grandpa needed to study the microbe more.

a Right   **b** Wrong   **c** Doesn't say

3 Grandpa was very tired after studying the microbe.

a Right   **b** Wrong   **c** Doesn't say

4 The gas in the tanker was called Shop Happy.

a Right   **b** Wrong   **c** Doesn't say

5 Happy World planned to sell the gas to people.

a Right   **b** Wrong   **c** Doesn't say

6 When people breathe the gas, they feel happy.

a Right   **b** Wrong   **c** Doesn't say

7 When people are happy they spend less money.

a Right   **b** Wrong   **c** Doesn't say

8 Alice was worried about Max and Rosie.

a Right   **b** Wrong   **c** Doesn't say

Talk **Why aren't Alice, Ben, and Grandpa laughing?**
Tell a friend your ideas.

Activities for pages 16–17

1 Choose the correct answers.

1 Why did Grandpa think that they didn't need a cure?

   a It was too difficult to make.

   b The gas was safe.

   (c) Rick stopped laughing.

   d Ben and Alice weren't laughing.

2 Why did Rick think that they still needed a cure?

   a His blood cells couldn't kill the microbes.

   b He was very tired.

   c He had stopped laughing.

   d Laughter is just the start of the illness.

3 Why did Rick stop laughing before Rosie?

   a He breathed the gas before Rosie.

   b Rosie was younger than Rick.

   c He had more white blood cells than Rosie.

   d He had a cure, but Rosie didn't.

4 How did Rosie feel when she stopped laughing?

   a Happy and safe

   b Sad and sick

   c Fine, but worried

   d OK, but tired

◎ **Activities** for pages 18–19

1 Find and write the words.

1 We get this from the ground or from
   the sea. We put it on our food.   s _ _ _

2 This is a type of illness.   c _ _ _

3 This is what you do with your mouth
   when you are tired.   y _ _ _

4 This describes a person that
   has an illness.   s _ _ _

5 We go _____ in water.   s _ _ _ _ _ _

6 We use this to kill an illness in the body.   c _ _ _

7 This describes a person who is sleeping.   a _ _ _ _ _

8 This is what you do with your nose
   when you have a cold.   s _ _ _ _ _

2 Circle the correct words.

1 Grandpa had a cold a few **weeks** / **days** ago.

2 **Alice** / **Rosie** had a cold, too.

3 Grandpa said that he could make a **cold** / **cure**.

4 Alice, Grandpa, and **Rosie** / **Clunk** worked hard.

5 Alice helped Grandpa to find **illnesses** / **chemicals**.

6 Grandpa needed lots of **salt** / **gas**.

7 They needed Ben to **make** / **get** some salt.

🗨 **Can Ben get the salt? Tell a friend your ideas.**

Activities for pages 20–21

1 **Decide if the sentences are** *correct* **(A) or** *incorrect* **(B).**

1 Everybody in the town was asleep.	Ⓐ	B
2 Ben had never felt so alone.	A	B
3 Ben had persuaded Max to come home.	A	B
4 Suddenly Ben heard his cell phone.	A	B
5 Grandpa told Ben that he needed a little bit of salt.	A	B
6 Ben was far from a supermarket.	A	B
7 Ben didn't pay for the bag of salt.	A	B
8 The bag of salt was heavy.	A	B
9 Ben could hear a man's voice on the phone.	A	B
10 The man sounded worried.	A	B

2 **Order the events.**

Ben left some money at the till.	_____
Ben couldn't wake Max up.	_1_
The shouts on the phone got louder.	_____
Ben put the bag of salt on his shoulder.	_____
Ben talked to Grandpa on his cell phone.	_____
Ben could hear a man's voice on the phone.	_____
Ben went to a supermarket.	_____

1 Choose and write the correct words.

Rick Richards had ¹_____ up and was ²_____.
He was angry and his face ³_____ redder. He thought
Clunk ⁴_____ trying to steal his ⁵_____. Rick
jumped ⁶_____ and ran at Clunk. Anger ⁷_____
be the next part of the ⁸_____! Clunk locked Rick in a
little room ⁹_____ the laboratory. Grandpa asked Ben
to get ¹⁰_____ quickly.

1   **a** woken   **b** waking   **c** wake   **d** woke

2   **a** shouts   **b** shouted   **c** shouting   **d** shout

3   **a** could   **b** got   **c** was   **d** had

4   **a** was   **b** had   **c** didn't   **d** wasn't

5   **a** job   **b** work   **c** worker   **d** company

6   **a** on   **b** to   **c** at   **d** up

7   **a** must   **b** could   **c** should   **d** would

8   **a** ill   **b** feel ill   **c** illness   **d** sick

9   **a** next   **b** next to   **c** next at   **d** next of

10   **a** homes   **b** house   **c** homely   **d** home

Activities for pages 24–25

1 Who said this? Write the names.

1 'You must fight it!' _Alice_

2 'Why's everyone on the ground?' _____

3 '… now I have the laughing illness, too.' _____

4 'Aren't you worried about Ben?' _____

5 'Stop that boy! He's stealing something!' _____

6 'I *had* a cold a few days ago, but it has almost gone.' _____

7 'Then … why are you smiling?' _____

2 Match. Then write the sentences.

1 The smile didn't   • almost gone.

2 Grandpa's cold had   • the laughing illness.

3 The microbe took   • the laughing illness, too.

4 But now Grandpa had   • leave Grandpa's face.

5 Grandpa had to fight   • longer to grow in Grandpa.

1 _The smile didn't leave Grandpa's face._

2 _____

3 _____

4 _____

5 _____

1 **Choose the best answers.**

1 Worker: Hey, come back here!

   Ben: __f__

2 Worker: You can't take that bag of salt.

   Ben: _____

3 Worker: Where are you taking it?

   Ben: _____

4 Worker: Where is your grandpa?

   Ben: _____

5 Worker: What is he going to do with the salt?

   Ben: _____

---

a He needs me to help him.

b But I left some money by the till!

c My grandpa has the laughing illness.

d He's at home.

e I'm not sure. But he asked me to get it for him.

f I can't. I need to get home.

g It won't take long.

h I need to take it to my grandpa.

Talk **Can Ben get home to Grandpa? Tell a friend your ideas.**

Activities for pages 28–29

1 Choose the correct answers.

1 Why was Alice getting more and more frightened?

   a Rosie was still sleeping.

   b Rick Richards was hitting the door.

   c Clunk was mixing the chemicals.

   d Grandpa had the laughing illness.

2 Why were Grandpa's hands shaking?

   a He was mixing the chemicals.

   b He was so tired.

   c He didn't want to go to sleep.

   d He was laughing so much.

3 What did Clunk do?

   a He laughed so much he couldn't speak.

   b He added the salt to the other chemicals.

   c He told Ben what to do.

   d He tried to talk to Alice.

4 Why did Rick Richards want Clunk?

   a He wanted Clunk to help Grandpa.

   b He wanted to get the cure.

   c He thought Clunk was stealing his ideas.

   d He thought Clunk was angry and dangerous.

Activities for pages 30–31

1 Read the sentences. Choose and write the correct words.

1 After that, a _____ things happened very quickly.

   a some   **b** number   **c** few

2 At last, Rosie _____ her eyes.

   a has opened   **b** opened   **c** opening

3 Grandpa's cure _____ kill the Shop Happy microbes.

   a might   **b** must   **c** would

4 Everyone would be better _____.

   a immediacy   **b** immediate   **c** immediately

5 Clunk was _____ to fly the van over the town.

   a going   **b** being   **c** doing

2 Complete the sentences.

air   ~~laughing~~   running   van   happening

1 Suddenly Grandpa stopped ___laughing___.

2 Rick Richards stopped _____ at Clunk.

3 Rosie didn't know what was _____.

4 Ten minutes later, Clunk was in the _____.

5 The van flew up into the _____.

Activities for pages 32–33

1 **Write *yes* or *no*.**

  1 In town, some people were ready to fight. _____

  2 Everybody saw Clunk flying the van. _____

  3 As soon as the van passed, everything changed. _____

  4 Max thought it had been a strange day. _____

  5 Max remembered everything that
    happened that day. _____

  6 Max's best friend is Clunk. _____

  7 Ben explained everything to Max. _____

  8 Max wanted to go shopping. _____

2 **Order the events.**

Suddenly everything changed. _____

Max told Ben that he hated shopping. _____

Max called Ben on his cell phone. _____

Clunk flew over the town in the van. _____

Ben told Max what had happened. _____

People in the town were ready to fight. _____

People didn't know why they were arguing. _____

Ben smiled. _____

Talk **Why did Ben ask Max if he wanted to go shopping?**
Tell a friend your ideas.

1 Decide if the sentences are *correct* (A) or *incorrect* (B).

  1 Rick wasn't sure if Grandpa would help him.   A   B

  2 Happy World was going to destroy Shop Happy.   A   B

  3 Rick wanted to make a new and better gas.   A   B

  4 Grandpa liked the idea of a new gas.   A   B

  5 Rosie thought that the idea was terrible.   A   B

  6 Using a gas like Shop Happy in a store is illegal.   A   B

  7 Grandpa phoned the police.   A   B

  8 Rick had an important job with Happy World.   A   B

  9 Rick decided to do what was right.   A   B

10 Alice wanted to watch a funny movie.   A   B

2 Who said this? Write the names.

  1 'I've laughed enough today!'

  2 'And happier people buy more things.'   _____

  3 'Then will you make a new, *better* gas?'   _____

  4 'If stores and towns use it, people will
     feel better.'   _____

  5 'There's a funny movie on TV.'   _____

  6 '*Everyone* will be happier.'   _____

  7 'I still have a cold.'   _____

Talk Do you like this story? Talk to a friend.

Illness Research

1 **Complete the table with the words from the story.**

microbes   moustache   a cold   eyes   face   voice
hurt   head   stomach   sick   white blood cells
finger   cure   DNA   breathe   sneeze   hands
chemicals   ear   cough   feet   tired   better

Illness	The Body

Talk **Compare your table with a friend's. Are your tables similar or different? Can you add more words to your table?**

2 **Use the Internet to research these two illnesses. Make notes on each illness and then answer the questions.**

What is the name of the illness? _____ flu _____

What causes this illness?

_____

_____

_____

What happens to people with this illness?

_____

_____

Is there a cure for this illness?

_____

_____

What is the name of the illness? _____ hay fever _____

What causes this illness?

_____

_____

_____

What happens to people with this illness?

_____

_____

Is there a cure for this illness?

_____

_____

Glossary

Here are some words used in this book, and you can check what they mean. Use a dictionary to check other new words.

accident *noun*
an event that happens unexpectedly and causes injury or damage

badge *noun*
a small piece of metal or plastic that you carry or wear to show who you are

basket *noun*
a container for holding or carrying things

breathe *verb*
to take in and let out air through your nose and mouth

cell *noun*
the smallest living thing

chemical *noun*
a thing that has been produced

cold *noun*
an illness that causes sneezing, fever and headaches

company *noun*
a business that makes money by making or selling things

container *noun*
a box or bottle in which something can be put

cough *verb*
to force air suddenly and noisily through your throat

crowd *noun*
a large number of people gathered together

cure *noun*
something that makes an illness go away

destroy *verb*
to damage something so badly that it no longer exists

DNA *noun*
the chemicals in cells which carry information

doorway *noun*
an opening into a building or a room, where the door is

equipment *noun*
things that are needed for a particular activity

gas *noun*
a substance like air that is not a solid or a liquid

hole *noun*
a space in something solid

identity card *noun*
a card with a person's name and photograph on it that proves who they are

illegal *adjective*
not allowed by the law

knock *verb*
to hit something and make a noise

laughter *noun*
the sound of laughing

liquid *noun*
a substance that flows freely and is not a solid or a gas, for example, water

lock *verb*
to fasten something with a key

microbe *noun*
a tiny living thing